# PTSD

Healing for Bad Memories

Timothy S. Lane

New Growth Press

newgrowthpress.com

New Growth Press, Greensboro, NC 27401
newgrowthpress.com
Copyright © 2012 by Timothy S. Lane

Cover Design: Tandem Creative, Tom Temple, tandemcreative.net
Typesetting: Lisa Parnell, lparnell.com

ISBN-13: 978-1-938267-87-1
ISBN-13: 978-1-935273-74-5 (eBook)

Library of Congress Cataloging-in-Publication Data
Lane, Timothy S.
  PTSD : healing for bad memories / Timothy S. Lane.
    p. cm.
  Includes bibliographical references and index.
  ISBN-13: 978-1-938267-87-1 (alk. paper)
  1. Post-traumatic stress disorder—Religious aspects—Christianity.
  2. Psychic trauma—Religious aspects—Christianity. I. Title.
  BV4910.45.L36    2012
  248.8'61968521—dc23
                                                          2012026568

Printed in India

30 29 28 27 26 25 24 23        12 13 14 15 16

*To those who know that*
*there are no easy answers,*
*yet relying on Jesus*
*to show forth his glory in weakness,*
*you are my heroes.*

The LORD is a refuge for the oppressed,
    a stronghold in times of trouble.
Those who know your name will trust in you,
    for you, LORD, have never forsaken those
    who seek you.

                (Psalm 9:9–10)

You may have picked up this minibook because you or someone you know is struggling with Post-Traumatic Stress Disorder (PTSD). There are many aspects to this struggle and many great resources available. This minibook will focus on describing PTSD and, if you are suffering with PTSD, assisting you to take some basic steps toward growth in grace.

To understand a bit of the experience of PTSD, let's begin with a simple example. Years ago, I was driving about sixty down a rural road when I suddenly realized I had flown through an intersection with a blinking red stoplight. The crossroad only had a flashing yellow light. About 500 yards past the intersection, I pulled the car over in a cold sweat. As I started to drive again, I could not stop dwelling on what could have happened. If there had been a car coming down the other road, I could have been killed. The thought stayed with me for several hours, but within a day, it began to fade. Soon I was driving as if nothing had occurred.

Most people have had similar experiences. But what if something much more severe happens to you and the memory doesn't fade? What if it was something that was so traumatic it continues to affect your entire life for months and possibly years? Consider the following stories:

- Joey was eight when rising floodwaters nearly swept away his home. He and his family were rescued and taken to safety. Seven years later he is still afraid whenever it rains. He rarely leaves his house if it looks like a heavy downpour is on its way.

- Monica was in an abusive dating relationship when she was in college. Verbal and emotional manipulation by her ex-boyfriend left her fearful of relationships with men in general. After much counseling, she married a caring and gentle husband. But even after six months of marriage, she still has trouble sleeping. Her life is characterized by a pronounced feeling of being out of control. She is uninterested in sex and feels guilty for the way she treats her husband.
- John has just returned from a tour of duty in the military. During his service he witnessed a number of deaths and barely escaped serious harm when a roadside IED exploded a few hundred yards from his vehicle. Immediately after the explosion, he was too startled to help those who were injured. He has recurring nightmares of the events, and he struggles with guilt because he didn't help "fast enough." He feels guilty that he escaped and is alive. Since his return home, he's been having trouble eating, sleeping, and even talking to family and friends.

## What Is Post-Traumatic Stress Disorder or PTSD?

While each of these examples is different, Joey, Monica, and John are struggling with something called Post-Traumatic Stress Disorder (PTSD).[1] *PTSD is a persistent inability to deal with a traumatic event from the past to the extent that an individual's current lifestyle and other relationships are negatively impacted.*[2] PTSD is an official disorder that has been discussed and written about since the latter part of the nineteenth century.[3]

## How Can You Tell If You Are Experiencing PTSD?

Have you lived through a scary and dangerous event? Did that event happen more than a month ago? Do some of the following statements describe your feelings and actions since the event happened?

- Sometimes, all of a sudden, I feel like the event is happening again. I never know when this will occur.
- I have nightmares and bad memories of the terrifying event.
- I stay away from places, activities, and people that remind me of the event.
- I jump and feel upset when something happens without warning.
- I have a hard time trusting or feeling close to other people.
- I get angry easily.
- I feel guilty because others died and I lived.
- I feel mental and physical stress (sickness, panic attacks) when I talk about the event.
- I have trouble sleeping and my muscles are tense.[4]

If even a few of these statements describe you, you may be experiencing what is called PTSD. If you are, you already know that it is painful and debilitating. One of the most troubling aspects of PTSD is that, despite the passing of time, the fears do not go away. You might also have noticed that your fears often seem to get in the way of having normal, trusting relationships.

Typical problematic responses to trauma include the following: shame and guilt, a feeling that things are out of control, depression, anxiety, hostility, grief over loss, impulsive behaviors, body pains like headaches, over-compensation to regain a sense of control, self-mutilation,[5] avoidance, numbing, and changes in personality, just to name a few.[6] Some people's symptoms appear immediately, but for others they appear years later.

Sometimes those with PTSD unsuccessfully attempt to avoid their persistent traumatic memories by using drugs or alcohol to numb the pain, or by engaging in other forms of self-destructive behavior.[7]

PTSD can be the result of witnessing someone being badly injured or killed and is often associated with those who have been in military combat. But the most common traumatic events that lead to PTSD are rape and sexual abuse.[8] Not everyone who experiences a traumatic event will develop PTSD, but if you are struggling with it, you are not alone. Percentages vary, but about 40 percent of Americans have experienced at least one major trauma. Of those who have experienced some form of trauma, about 8 to 12 percent experience PTSD at some point in their lives.[9] It is estimated that more than 5.2 million Americans suffer with PTSD.

## The Intrusion of the Past into the Present

The symptoms of PTSD reveal a memory that struggles to stay in the past. A traumatic memory becomes detached (dissociated) from its identity as an event locked in the past and takes on a life of its own in the present. The memory then persistently intrudes into the present in debilitating ways by distorting what is currently happening.

If you struggle with PTSD, a present circumstance that even mildly resembles a trauma you've experienced might cause you to lose any distinction between your traumatic memory and your present situation. For example, someone who was physically or sexually assaulted will commonly become extremely defensive in a relationship that is not abusive. This blurring of the past and present is not limited to overt sexual or physical abuse. In another example, a woman who had been abused by previous church leaders through their mishandling of authority reacted with anger and defensiveness when her current leaders came and offered her help. This trigger created a deep fear in her that blinded her to the truth.

Triggers that remind a person of past trauma tend to be specific to each person. They can include sights, sounds, smells, tastes, significant dates or seasons, or an environment similar to where the trauma took place, among others.[10]

## Hope for PTSD Sufferers

It is important to know that struggling with PTSD does not make you abnormal or strange. It is quite understandable to struggle the way you do. In fact, it is amazing that people don't struggle more considering the significant suffering and trauma that some have endured.

While these symptoms, habits, and responses can be consuming and powerful, they are not too strong to break. As you will see, you can grow and change as you face your fears, seek help, and find hope and strength in God's powerful grace.

## Understanding Technical Labels

Because your suffering has the technical label of Post-Traumatic Stress Disorder, you might think that you are dealing with something that God does not really talk about in the Bible. But do not be intimidated by the label. PTSD, even within secular studies, is placed within the broader category of anxiety disorders such as generalized anxiety disorder, panic attacks, and obsessive-compulsive disorder. In simple terms, this is the biblical category of fear.

It is also important to realize that it is understandable for someone to struggle with deep fears after experiencing a traumatic event. People who struggle with PTSD and those who know them often see this struggle as odd, when in fact it is not. Fear running amok and expressing itself in extreme behaviors can be confusing and intimidating to both the PTSD sufferer and those who are close to the person.

Once you have located the struggle in this biblical category, the Bible comes alive! You have experienced a horrifying event or series of events and now you are afraid. Read any part of the Bible, and you will see that horrific, traumatic events have been part of the world since the fall of humanity into sin and suffering. Life in this world is full of trauma, suffering, and hurt. Yet it is within this context that the God of grace meets people and gives them hope, comfort, and courage to face the uncertainties of life.

## You See an Aspect of Reality that Many Ignore

In some ways your traumatic experience has made you more realistic about how fragile life is. Many people live as though nothing bad will ever happen to them—as if they are invincible. But God says that this type of thinking is foolish and arrogant. James 4:13–16 says,

> Now listen, you who say, "Today or tomorrow we will go to this or that city, spend a year there, carry on business and make money." Why, you do not even know what will happen tomorrow. What is your life? You are a mist that appears for a little while and then vanishes. Instead, you ought to say, "If it is the Lord's will, we will live and do this or that." As it is, you boast and brag. All such boasting is evil.

James is saying that your sense that life is fragile and precarious is actually an aspect of wisdom. But what do you do with that insight? You do not have to be overcome with fear and worry. The Scripture has much to say to you in the middle of your struggle.

## Begin by Crying Out to God

When God speaks to his people, he doesn't gloss over the discord and misery of life. The Bible is not Pollyannaish when it comes to life in a broken world. In fact, if you are struggling with PTSD, the Bible is the book that should most intrigue and comfort you. Start by looking at Psalm 27, written by Israel's second king, David. You might think you would have little in common with him, but he, like you, lived in a disturbing world of hostility and hurt. Read his words and see if they express some of your feelings.

> When evil men advance against me to devour
> my flesh, when my enemies and my foes attack
> me, they will all stumble and fall. Though
> an army besiege me, my heart will not fear;
> though war break out against me, even then
> will I be confident. . . . Though my father and
> mother forsake me, the LORD will receive me.
> (Psalm 27:2–3, 10)

Perhaps you also have felt assailed and forsaken as David did long ago. Like you, David lived in violent times. He was in danger from his enemies and even his own family. In your struggle with trauma, you can find strength in knowing you are not alone. Even more than that, you can find strength in crying out your trouble to God the way David did. In the midst of his traumatic reality, David never stopped crying out to God for help. David lived wisely. He knew his life could be cut short in a minute so he lived in dependent humility upon God's grace and protection. Listen to how David cried to God.

> Hear my voice when I call, O LORD; be
> merciful to me and answer me. My heart says
> of you "Seek his face!" Your face, LORD, I will

seek. Do not hide your face from me, do not
turn your servant away in anger; you have
been my helper. Do not reject me or forsake
me, O God my Savior. (Psalm 27:7–9)

## Before You Get Discouraged by the Bible . . .

Before you start comparing your life and reaction to
trauma with David's, it is important that you read this
psalm through an accurate lens. First, David wrote this
psalm as an example of what is possible when the Spirit
of God is powerfully at work in someone's life. David
was writing this in the context of spiritual growth. He
also struggled and experienced days when he did not
faithfully trust God. Read Psalm 51 and you will see that
David experienced significant moral failure and he con-
fessed sins and shortcomings from a particular moment
in his life. David showed you what is possible, but he did
not tell you it is easy.

Also, as you read any psalm or passage in the Bible,
it ultimately points you to Jesus. David was a king, but
he was not a perfect king. The perfect king is Jesus.
David was a signpost pointing to a greater king than
himself. When you read Psalm 27, remember that you
have a great king who has suffered in your place and
understands what you are going through. He also laid
his life down for your failures and lived a perfect life
on your behalf, so that you could be fully reconciled
to God and experience his complete forgiveness and
love. No doubt, you will struggle and fail, but you
are related to someone who understands, forgives, and

provides grace and strength to grow in faith and obedience. Read this psalm, and any other, through this lens.

## David Remembers God's Mercy, and You Can Too

David begs God to listen to him, help him, and be with him in trouble. But he doesn't stop there. He goes on to remember and focus on God's mercy to him right now.

> One thing I ask of the LORD, this is what I seek: that I may dwell in the house of the LORD all the days of my life, to gaze upon the beauty of the LORD and to seek him in his temple. For in the day of trouble he will keep me safe in his dwelling; he will hide me in the shelter of his tabernacle and set me high upon a rock. Then my head will be exalted above the enemies who surround me; at his tabernacle will I sacrifice with shouts of joy; I will sing and make music to the LORD. (Psalm 27:4–6)

David turns from his experience of hurt and violence toward God. He experiences God's mercy as he directs his gaze to God and seeks his presence. For David, God's presence could be found and seen in God's house, his tabernacle. In the Old Testament, God's tabernacle was the place where God's presence was symbolically represented. It was also the place where the high priest sacrificed and made intercession for sins. Remember the lens we talked about above that teaches us to read the Bible

13

with Christ in mind. We have an even greater high priest to rely upon—Jesus, who lives forever. Looking for and remembering God's presence simply means filling your mind and heart with Jesus Christ and talking to him as your Redeemer. Hebrews 4:14–16 helps us understand what this looks like.

> Since then we have a great high priest who has passed through the heavens, Jesus, the Son of God, let us hold fast our confession. For we do not have a high priest who is unable to sympathize with our weaknesses, but one who in every respect has been tempted as we are, yet without sin. Let us then with confidence draw near to the throne of grace, that we may receive mercy and find grace to help in time of need. (ESV)

Cultivating a memory that allows the great mercy of God to overshadow your trauma is a lifelong battle. But you have a high priest who sympathizes with your weakness. You have a high priest who also experienced traumatic suffering. When you go to God, you are going to the One who understands your suffering and knows just how to help you. Isaiah 53 and Hebrews 2 are just two places where you will find pictures of how Jesus has identified with you in your sufferings. Allow these passages and others like them to help you talk to God. He is not a lifeless object but a personal God who enters into relationship with his children.

## Present Hope Is Grounded in the Resurrection

Jesus' suffering and death was not the end. He also rose from the dead. His resurrection is your guarantee that if you trust in Jesus you will also one day be resurrected. No matter what sad and hard things you experience in this world, one day all your sorrow and suffering will be swept away. At the end of Psalm 27, David looks forward to the future God has for him by saying, "I am still confident of this: I will see the goodness of the LORD in the land of the living. Wait for the LORD; be strong and take heart and wait for the LORD" (Psalm 27:13–14). Unlike David, we have a much bigger understanding of our future hope since the coming of Jesus. This hope is not just a promise for the future. The implications for Jesus' resurrection have present benefits. Take comfort in these verses from Ephesians 1:18–21.

> I pray also that the eyes of your heart may be enlightened in order that you may know the hope to which he has called you, the riches of his glorious inheritance in the saints, and his incomparably great power for us who believe. That power is like the working of his mighty strength, which he exerted in Christ when he raised him from the dead and seated him at his right hand in the heavenly realms, far above all rule and authority, power and dominion, and every title that can be given, not only in the present age but also in the one to come.

Paul wants his brothers and sisters in Christ to know that there is a new power at work in them right now and it is tied to Jesus' resurrection. Verse 19 says that this great power is at work in those who believe in the present. Not only is there a promise to one day be rid of the suffering, there is a present promise that you are being made new and that God's power is at work in you now.[11] There are significant victories in the present that can be encouraging to the sufferer and to those witnessing the power of God's grace at work in those who have suffered significantly.

## Remember the Vastness of the Gospel

Jesus' life, death, resurrection, ascension, gift of the Spirit, intercession for you, and his promised return provide you with powerful reasons to rivet your attention on what God has done, is doing, and will do for you. The truths of the gospel are the only substantive reality that can reshape your memory and speak into your trauma. Jesus came to this earth and died for you. When you put your trust in him, you can be assured that you will never be alone or forsaken. You can be sure that all the promises that David believed are yours. You can be sure you are God's dearly loved child. The apostle John explains it like this:

> How great is the love the Father has lavished on
> us, that we should be called children of God!
> And that is what we are! The reason the world
> does not know us is that it did not know him.

Dear friends, now we are children of God, and
what we will be has not yet been made known.
But we know that when he appears, we shall be
like him, for we shall see him as he is. Everyone
who has this hope in him purifies himself, just
as he is pure. (1 John 3:1–3)

Acknowledging and believing your future resurrection and who you are as a child of God will enable you to
move forward each day. You will grow in peace and stability as you interact with God in light of this profound
relationship you have with him. Christian change is not
a cognitive exercise where you replace falsehood with
truth. It is not less than that, but it is so much more. A
Christian's growth is based upon an actual relationship
that you have with a personal, redeeming God.

## Practical Strategies for Change
*I don't want to remember, but I can't seem to forget.*
PTSD sufferer[12]

### Seeking a Skilled, Godly Helper
Most of the time, it is imperative that you find someone who has experience helping people with serious
trauma.[13] While your brothers and sisters in Christ play
an important part in your growth in grace, you will
likely need the help of a professional who has wisdom
and experience dealing with this type of problem. Don't
be afraid to ask for help. Reading this minibook may be
the first time you have tried to get help and that is a good

first step. Next you need to know that it is okay and important to ask for help from someone else.

When you seek help from a pastor or a counselor, do not be afraid to ask them what experience they have. *You will want someone who allows you to be honest about your struggles but makes you feel safe at the same time.* If you are not careful and you begin to process memories with someone who is not skilled enough, it could make things worse. You need a great deal of guidance in the early stages, so do not hurry to find the best person. You want a person who understands the fragility of life and believes that in the midst of uncertainty God is our refuge and strength and an ever-present help in times of trouble (Psalms 46 and 121). You want someone who is going to guide you to find comfort in the life, sufferings, death, and resurrection of Jesus. You want someone who is patient and understands that the change process takes time. So look carefully for a skilled helper.

## What Are Your Expectations?

The path of change is rarely quick and easy. There are times when God works in immediate ways, but most often the change process takes time. There will be days when you see good movement and days when you will wonder if anything has changed. Don't be deceived into thinking that because of this ebb and flow pattern of change you are somehow uniquely troubled. Remember, this is true of every struggle with sin and suffering. Every believer, no matter what the issue, is in a process of lifelong change that includes good days and difficult days. God is ever patient with his children, and his love for you is persistent not sporadic (Ephesians 1:1–14; John 10:1–18).

## Learning to Cultivate New Memories and Reintegrate the Past Trauma

We will use Psalm 27 as a model of the process of change and growth. While we can't say that David was experiencing PTSD, we can learn from David's life and growth in grace. One thing David does in this psalm (as in many others) is place hardship, suffering, and traumatic events within an integrated whole that includes God's goodness and mercy. The traumatic events are not dissociated or isolated from God's saving mercies. In addition, David expresses a wide range of emotion that includes sadness as well as gratitude and joy. David is living as a whole man within the context of an integrated understanding of suffering and blessing. This life did not come to David overnight; it was a process. This is good news because we can hope for the same in our own lives.

The memory of your trauma can be so overwhelming that you feel like you are stuck in the past. That is why it is imperative to fill your mind with realities that are equally, if not more, penetrating than your trauma. Meditating on and remembering God's redeeming grace and relating to him on this basis will gradually demote your trauma and promote God's care for you. This will most likely be a slow process, but as you do this daily, you will gain greater stability. If you are afraid to cry out to God, it is helpful to have someone walk with you as you learn to interact with him.

Here is some practical guidance for what this might look like. Take Psalm 27 and make it into your own psalm as you relate to God. Read the whole psalm through and then take a piece of paper and rewrite it so that it expresses your life and your experience specifically. Invite someone to help you do this. Use the following three points to guide your writing:

1. *Cry out to God with your thoughts and feelings.* Just as David did, go to God and tell him all about your struggles, your fear, your anxiety, and your guilt. The Christian life covers the entire spectrum of emotion. This is an essential aspect of being made in God's image. Cry out to God for help. Notice how many things David asks God for in this psalm. You can ask him for the exact same things. Simple cries for help and assistance are significant in your struggle. Direct your cries to God, even if all you can express is desperation. God hears and acts when he hears even the feeblest cry for help from his children.

2. *Remember God and his mercy to you.* When your mind is riveted on a past traumatic experience, put that past event within the bigger context of who God is and who you are in relationship to him. This is where you will find safety and help. Look through Psalm 27 and write down all the things David says are true about God. Then pray through your list, thanking God for who he is and what he has done. Pray that God's Spirit will fill you so

that you know the truth of God's faithfulness and love for you. Why isn't David afraid when an army surrounds him (Psalm 27:3)? How does God help David? Can you remember and write down some ways that God's help has come to you? Remember, you know even more about God's mercy than David did. You know about Jesus' life, death, and resurrection. Think about what it means to have a Redeemer who understands you and loves you so much he died for you.

3. *Locate your hope in God and his resurrection power.* What fills David with hope in this psalm? Where does that hope come from? Rewrite the verses that express hope in your own words. How does Jesus' resurrection bring hope to you?

There are many other Bible passages you could do this exercise with. Psalm 118 repeats the phrase "for His mercy endures forever" (NKJV) as the psalmist remembers all of God's powerful saving acts for Israel. You could rewrite that psalm and remember God's mercy and love for you. You could also read and memorize Philippians 2:1–11. As you do so, recount and remember God's power and saving acts in Jesus' life, death, and resurrection. The Bible is full of people who grew in grace as they faced trauma of all kinds. They grew because they cried out to God, and he helped them. As you cry out to God, he will help you too. Do not do this just once. Keep going to God. Keep crying out to him. Keep remembering his mercy and the hope of resurrection. Keep filling your mind and heart with the hope of the whole gospel.

## Living in Community

Psalm 27 tells us that while David is in the temple he not only remembers God's mercy, but he also finds others gathered there who are in desperate need of mercy just like him. Like David, you need to face your struggle in a community of faith. There is no replacement for life in God's community. In popular literature on PTSD, living in meaningful relationships with others is always mentioned as a vital part of change. Find a community of believers who are skilled at creating an environment of honesty and safety.[14]

This can be tricky for someone who struggles with past trauma. Typically, because the person is fearful of others, they often do things in relationships that make it hard for others to relate to them. In addition, people trying to help someone with PTSD can often get frustrated and even angry because they don't see as much change as they would like. Sadly, this scenario is quite common.

A mark of maturity in someone who has PTSD will be seen in the way they alert people to their struggles. Alerting others that their fear can drive them to be demanding or defensive will assist well-intentioned helpers to be patient. Wise helpers should also be growing in their ability to ask about a person's history so that they can determine whether the individual is currently affected by traumatic events. People who struggle with PTSD can be misunderstood by well-intentioned helpers and end up "re-traumatized" when the helpers become frustrated or angry.

Are there people in your church with whom you can spend time? Is there a wise helper, perhaps even someone who might have a similar struggle with PTSD? Look for a Christian counselor who will assist you as you walk down this path. If you don't know anyone, ask around. Go talk to a pastor or someone in leadership at your church. Don't wait for those around you to notice that you are suffering. Move toward others and seek help. In the same way that you are to move toward God because of his mercy, move toward others who can be conduits of God's mercy to you. Remember, God is moving toward you and is graciously pursuing you even when you are not pursuing him or his people. He is that committed to you! He leaves the ninety-nine to go after the one.

Ask a few friends to pray for you regularly and invite them to check how you are doing. Find ways to fill your mind with the truths of God's goodness and power. Some people find music to be a powerful source of meditation. Are there songs that lead you to find comfort and hope in God's grace and strength? It can be helpful to meditate on God's work in creation. In Psalm 19, the psalmist not only finds hope in God's truth, he sees God's glory in the beauty of creation. Living in community means you are seeking to move out and serve others. Make simple steps to move toward others even when you are struggling. God honors humble service to others even when done in weakness.

There are no easy answers and quick fixes to your experience of trauma. But as you persevere in moving toward God and others in the midst of your trouble, God will meet you, help you, and transform you.

## Pursue the Option of Medication Wisely

Post-Traumatic Stress Disorder is a particularly difficult form of suffering because it seems to go on and on, and it can dominate your life. The Bible teaches that we are one person with two aspects, body (outer person) and soul (inner person), so it should not surprise us when we find the one influencing the other (Genesis 2:7). If you are suffering with the symptoms of PTSD, be willing to seek a medical assessment and stay open to the possibility of using medication.[15] Medication will not solve your problem, but it may help you function well enough to benefit from wise and godly counsel.

Yet, since the Bible also says you have a soul, you must look deeper than the physiological symptoms of anxiety that you are experiencing. PTSD doesn't happen in a vacuum; it happens to people who have a personality and a history.

Start asking questions that address what is happening in your soul in the midst of your struggle. What do your fears and worries reveal about what is most important to you? What do you want most from life? Where are you dissatisfied with your relationship with God? How is this suffering revealing ways that God is currently at work or wants to work in your life? Celebrate that work; don't minimize it! With a solid foundation in God's accepting grace, these types of questions can be raised in positive ways. I would recommend that you do this with another person who can encourage you when you are discouraged.

## Face Your Doubts of God's Goodness Honestly

When people have experienced severe trauma, it often leads them to question God's goodness, power, and wisdom. But how can you move toward God when you find yourself doubting whether he is safe or will keep you safe? Again, he is always moving toward you, and he understands your questions and doubts.

Because you have experienced a traumatic event, your doubts and questions are understandable. In fact, not to ask questions might be a sign of denial. Offering and accepting platitudes and pious advice as you struggle with the reality of injustice and suffering in our world will only make your struggle harder.

The Bible does not answer all of your questions with specific details. But that doesn't mean God doesn't have answers for you. Nor does it mean he doesn't care. When Scripture addresses the problem of evil and injustice in the world, it speaks of something that no other world philosophy or religion can. It points us to a God who suffered.

> In bringing many sons to glory, it was fitting
> that God, for whom and through whom
> everything exists, should make the author of
> their salvation perfect through suffering. . . .
> Since the children have flesh and blood, he too

shared in their humanity so that by his death he might destroy him who holds the power of death—that is, the devil—and free those who all their lives were held in slavery by their fear of death. For surely it is not angels he helps, but Abraham's descendants. For this reason he had to be made like his brothers in every way, in order that he might become a merciful and faithful high priest in service to God, and that he might make atonement for the sins of the people. Because he himself suffered when he was tempted, he is able to help those who are being tempted. (Hebrews 2:10, 14–18)

The apostle John says, "This is how we know what love is: Jesus Christ laid down his life for us" (1 John 3:16).

The Bible also reminds us repeatedly that one day God will address all of the injustice in the world. He does not promise to do this according to our timeframe, but according to his. Romans 8:18–39, 1 Corinthians 15, and the entire book of Revelation are just some of the verses where God reminds us that nothing will escape his justice. At the end of the book of Revelation, the apostle John says the following about our final destiny:

Then I saw a new heaven and a new earth, for the first heaven and the first earth had passed away, and the sea was no more. And I saw the Holy City, new Jerusalem, coming down out of heaven from God, prepared, as a bride adorned for her husband. And I heard a loud voice from the throne saying, "Behold, the dwelling place of God is with man. He will dwell with them, and they will be his people, and God himself will be with them as their God. He will wipe away every tear from their eyes, and death shall be no more, neither shall there be mourning, nor crying, nor pain anymore, for the former things have passed away." And *he who was seated on the throne said, "Behold, I am making all things new."* Revelation 21:1–5 (ESV, emphasis added)

John's vision of all suffering being ended is not meant to make us bury our heads in the sand, deny the existence of evil and injustice in the world, and sit silently as passive bystanders. Instead, it is meant to give us confidence that as we work against the evil in this world, our hope is not in what we can do but in what God is doing and will do. God wants us to join him in fighting against evil wherever we see it (Ephesians 6) with deeds of justice, kindness, grace, and sacrifice. At the same time he invites us to trust the outcome of the battle to him. God does care, he is powerful, and he is *personally* involved in our suffering.

## Facing Your "Survivor's Guilt"

Another aspect of PTSD is the stress that occurs after someone witnesses a traumatic event. You may have seen a traumatic event, but escaped harm yourself. Suppose you were a soldier and one of your fellow soldiers was killed while you were on a mission together. Survivor's guilt is not uncommon. You may wonder why it happened to them and not you, and the guilt is overwhelming.

Feelings of guilt after witnessing a traumatic event are more pronounced the closer one is to the person who experienced the trauma. For parents, these feelings may be particularly acute. At one level, the trauma you experienced has put you more in touch with reality. No one lives a life free of suffering. It's amazing that even more traumatic events don't happen. That they don't is a sign of God's grace. Still, you have been shaken, and you can't ignore what has happened. God wants you to know that he is with you and committed to you in the midst of your guilt.

But how do you deal with your guilt? Begin by recognizing that your guilt is tapping into something deeper. It may be revealing something about what you think you deserve or don't deserve based upon a worldview that fails to recognize that terrible things happen to Christians too. This is hard to acknowledge, but your assumptions about your safety can't be rooted in a sense that you deserve more or less than what happens to others. If your neighbors receive blessings, the temptation is jealousy. If they receive suffering or hardship, the temptation might be relief or possibly guilt. But look at all the difficulty that happened to people in the Bible: Moses, Abraham, Paul, and Jesus himself suffered greatly!

A foundation that says that you get blessing or hardship based on your own failures or successes will tend to move you toward either jealousy or guilt. However, if your foundation is the grace of God, when someone

28

receives blessing you can rejoice and when someone receives difficulty, you can mourn and grieve without the debilitating pangs of guilt. When God's free grace is prominent, guilt doesn't make sense.

Paul encouraged us to "rejoice with those who rejoice; mourn with those who mourn" (Romans 12:15). Proper mourning is entirely appropriate for the Christian. But mourning should not be driven by guilt; mourning should be propelled by the reality that things are not the way they are supposed to be. Jesus says that mourning is one mark of someone who knows and loves God (Matthew 5:4). It is a sign of someone who is deeply aware of how broken this world is.

In the gospel of Luke, an account is recorded where others witnessed a very traumatic event. Notice the people's question and Jesus' response.

> There were some present at that very time who told him about the Galileans whose blood Pilate had mingled with their sacrifices. And he answered them, "Do you think that these Galileans were worse sinners than all the other Galileans, because they suffered in this way? No, I tell you; but unless you repent, you will all likewise perish. Or those eighteen on whom the tower in Siloam fell and killed them: do you think that they were worse offenders than all the others who lived in Jerusalem? No, I tell you; but unless you repent, you will all likewise perish." (Luke 13:1–5 ESV)

The first thing they ask Jesus is whether they were less sinful than those who were killed. But Jesus challenges this natural response. He answers the "who is more sinful?" question by pointing out that those who are still living aren't any better than those who died. Both the living and the dead need forgiveness equally.

## Find Help and Hope in the Midst of Your Suffering

PTSD is a serious and debilitating form of suffering. It can cripple a person's ability to live life, relate to others, or function with some measure of stability. *But it cannot prevent you from glorifying God.* It can make it more challenging and difficult, but it cannot render you incapable of loving God and others by his grace. In the midst of your suffering and struggle, Jesus is a very present help. He promises to walk with you and to make you more like him as you grow in grace. The apostle Peter wrote these words to fellow Christians who were facing severe and cruel persecution (trauma). Take heart as you continue to fight the good fight.

> Praise be to the God and Father of our Lord
> Jesus Christ! In his great mercy he has given
> us new birth into a living hope through the
> resurrection of Jesus Christ from the dead, and
> into an inheritance that can never perish,
> spoil or fade—kept in heaven for you, who
> through faith are shielded by God's power
> until the coming of the salvation that is ready

to be revealed in the last time. In this you greatly rejoice, though now for a little while you may have had to suffer grief in all kinds of trials. These have come so that your faith—of greater worth than gold, which perishes even though refined by fire—may be proved genuine and may result in praise, glory and honor when Jesus Christ is revealed. Though you have not seen him, you love him; and even though you do not see him now, you believe in him and are filled with an inexpressible and glorious joy, for you are receiving the goal of your faith, the salvation of your souls. (1 Peter 1:3–9)

## Endnotes

1. Studies show that there are differences between military combat trauma and trauma that happens to younger children by those in authority. Still, much overlap does exist.

2. Bradley D. Gringe, M.D., "Diagnosis and Management of Post-Traumatic Stress Disorder," *American Family Physician*: http://www.aafp.org/afp/2003/1215/p2401.html (December 2003). Also note Judith Herman, *Trauma and Recovery* (Basic Books, 1992). Herman traces PTSD studies back to the 1880s and sexual abuse committed against women.

3. Gringe, "Diagnosis and Management."

4. This list of symptoms is from the website of the National Institute of Mental Health at http://www.nimh.nih.gov/health/publications/post-traumatic-stress-disorder-ptsd/what-are-the-symptoms-of-ptsd.shtml.

5. For some, the act of self-mutilation or self-injury is an attempt to create new pain that diverts attention from the original trauma. The new pain is also easier to control and

gives the sufferer the feeling that this is something they can manage, unlike the original trauma.

6. Glenn R. Schiraldi, Ph.D., *The Post-Traumatic Stress Disorder Sourcebook: A Guide to Healing, Recovery, and Growth* (New York, McGraw-Hill, 2000), 26–35.

7. Ibid.

8. Gringe, "Diagnosis and Management."

9. Schiraldi, *The Post-Traumatic Stress Disorder Sourcebook*, 36.

10. Ibid., 17–20.

11. If not careful, the promise of the resurrection can be a strange rationale for someone to consider suicide: "If I end my life, I will not have to suffer like this anymore." It is important to infuse hope for the present and not just for the future.

12. Schiraldi, *The Post-Traumatic Stress Disorder Sourcebook*, 147.

13. In addition to *The Post-Traumatic Stress Disorder Sourcebook* by Schiraldi, another helpful resource is *The PTSD Workbook* by Mary Beth Williams and Soili Poijula. While neither of these is written from a Christian point of view, they do provide some helpful insights and practical tools that can be used when counseling someone with PTSD. Not everything will be helpful or even wise to use, but there is much to glean from these two resources.

14. Sadly, churches and helpers are not good at providing a context of honesty and safety where someone can struggle as they grow in grace. In fact, the church can act in such a way that they "re-traumatize" someone and reinforce the fearful person's sense of isolation.

15. Secular treatments for PTSD usually involve a combination of approaches, including group therapy, individual counseling, and medication, particularly the selective serotonin reuptake inhibitors (SSRI's). In more severe cases, antipsychotic medication is recommended.